EVENTUALLY

poems

Sydna Altschuler Byrne

Eventually

© 2020 by Sydna Altschuler Byrne

All rights reserved. No part of this book may be used or reproduced in any manner without written permission by the author except in critical articles or reviews.

ISBN: 978-1-951937-06-5
Library of Congress
Control Number 2020930928

Contact the publisher for information:
Epigraph Books
22 East Market Street, Suite 304
Rhinebeck, New York 12572
(845) 876-4861
www.epigraphps.com

Cover Photo: Ashfield, Ma. (by SAB)
Author Photo: Amy Scott Byrne
Cover Design: Nora Porter

*For family and friends
and those special moments of
love and inspiration*

CONTENTS

Eventually   1

What The Muse Said   3

Bird Feeder   4

When You Write   5

One Old Crow to Another   7

Trimming Cutoffs Made From
    Old Blue Jeans   8

Continuum   9

Haiku   10

Despite Summer's Heat   11

Paradox   12

Release   13

The Storyteller   14

The Woman on the Island   15

Tea for Two   16

Wildlife Via Canada   17

Night Dilemma I   19

Night Dilemma II   20

Dream Life   21

Shopping for Peaches   22

Firewood   23

On Seeing the Universe
    In a Blade of Grass   25

The Muted Town Crier   26

The Tapes   27

Famous Author Reads   29

Missed Photo Op # 1   30

Missed Photo Op # 2   31

Missed Photo Op # 3   32

How to Learn to Sing   33

How to Begin to Exercise   34

How to Begin to Write   35

How to Continue to Write   36

Writing Prompt   37

Sister Fear   38

On a Letter of Rejection   39

When I Was Eight   41

Whose Lint Between Her Toes   43

Lullaby   44

Grammar Lesson: To, Two, and Too   45

The Present   46

Elegy for My Father   47

Elegy for My Mother   49

Tree   51

To Be A Poet   52

About the Author   53

Whoever you are, no matter how lonely,
the world offers itself to your imagination...

> Mary Oliver
> *Wild Geese*

Is there a place for all the words
that don't want to stay? ...
These words that escape,
where do they lie in wait?

> Eduardo Galeano
> *Walking Words*

EVENTUALLY

Eventually

Eventually you will go on a journey
from which no one returns
except in memory

You will leave projects unfinished
books unread, music unheard
you will want to kiss your children

One more time
and your grandchildren
and friends and lovers

Because there was
a beginning
there will be an ending

For some it will come too early
for others painfully late
wait, wait as long as you can

Remember wet leaves, gold and red
on the windshield of your car
in the Fall air

Tell the leaves that you love them
clinging like happy children
enjoying the rain

Go when it is time
as children too must leave--
seeking other comforts, other joys

There will be moments when
all who knew you will remember
how you loved them

There will be such moments
Enjoy thinking about them
Then let them go

What The Muse Said

Did you see me right away?
I have been waiting in the wings for you
Perhaps you wonder if I am real

Loosen the curtain and touch me
then you will know

If I disappear, I will return
You will find me again
I will be waiting in the wings for you

Bird Feeder

Can you taste their colors?
    These red cardinals
        and black capped chickadees

Pecking at sunflower seeds
    and millet, their heads turning
        side to side

Can you feel their bright warmth
    warming your own breath
        while you

Give them
    all the bread you saved
        to spread over crusty snow

Your arms like clipped wings
    saved
        scattering bread

When You Write

Search for words
like a seagull
scanning for clam signs--
tiny breathing holes
in the sand

Feel words in your fingertips;
pull them out, touch their edges,
split them,
and if one won't open
fly up with it until you
think you've got the right height

then drop it on the rocks below
over and over again till it splits;
or let it lie;
even a gull gives up on a clam
that's sealed like stone.

Be not wed to one meaning alone;
a marriage where only the vows remain
cannot move with the tides.

Walk barefoot in your sand;
toes know where to find such treasures
half buried, barely defined;

Dig for them
Fly with them
Drop them, retrieve them

Collect them like shells,
Carry them in your pockets,
Play with them

Use words to mark your footprints
in the sand

Use them to make a meaning
no wave can erase.

One Old Crow to Another

You there on that bare branch
your feet wrapped around
feeling for a spring bud breaking
through the bark

Patience!
Nothing glistens now but this snow.
We won't see new life for a while

Patience!
Come, caw with me
Caw caw with me
Let us sing
and spring will come

Trimming Cutoffs Made From Old Blue Jeans

Note how one hand holds the threads
while the other holds the scissors
how easily the scissors work

how quickly the threads are cut
how you look out and
see a hummingbird

how this needle-beaked
       drinker of sweetness
              pierces your dark clouds

and lets the sun shine in
       lets the sun shine in
              sun shine in

Continuum

Birds perch on
telephone wires

They are the first
to hear the message

Something about a canary
in a coal mine

Haiku

A lawnmower roars

Then someone starts hammering

Wait! Listen! Birds Sing

Despite Summer's Heat

She wore a hat
Swirling to the lively music
Holding her laughing toddler--
Eyes locked on her child's face

The mother's hat covered
Nothing that mattered now
Wisps of down that would grow
It would grow

Like her toddler's hair
It would grow
They would grow together
They would dance some more

Paradox

When I am asleep
and do not know I am asleep
Sometimes I have dreams
in which I am awake

And when I am awake
and do not feel quite awake
     a pale yellow butterfly dances
         outside my kitchen window

and I wonder if I am dreaming

Release

The day they found the three year-old asleep
One sneaker on, a t-shirt, bare bottomed
Lost for two days in the woods
Trekking on his way toward grandmother's house

That day I remembered the tiny insect
Captive for days in a jar on the porch
Checkered black and gold
Clearly not the dreaded deer tick

That day I opened the jar
Saw the bug move one leg, then another
Gave it water
Tore off a corner of paper

Carried the bug outdoors on its paper carpet
Set it down beside some dead leaves
Rigid, unmoving until I provided a fresh green weed
Watched it climb onto that stalk

Like that little boy
Clinging to his rescuer's neck,
Asking for something to eat, to drink

The Storyteller

Think of a river the storyteller said
and I selected and discarded various
rivers until one remained and then
the storyteller said to picture a tree
near the river and I considered maple
and acorn and aspen and tulip and
evergreen until a weeping willow
settled in near my river and
the storyteller asked
if everyone had a river and a tree
in mind and we said yes and he asked
if we thought any of our rivers
were alike and we said no and he asked
if any of our trees were alike
and we said probably not and he said
therefore he was not the storyteller
but we were the storytellers
telling ourselves the story
choosing which river and which tree.

The Woman on the Island

The train stopped near a lake.
In the lake there was a small island.
On the island there were four trees,
two evergreens and two without leaves
and a woman. The woman on the train
waved hello to the woman on the island.
The woman on the island shouted hello
in return. The train began to move.
Whether the woman on the island
joined the woman on the train,
it is hard to say.
Or if the woman
on the train went to the island
it is also impossible to know
since the island seemed too small
to inhabit. And the woman on the train
appeared to be asleep.

Tea for Two

This is how I survive the cold
and wrap myself against the chill
I make tea and hold the tags
that connect the threads to the tea bags
one tag in each hand
dipping the bags up and down
one in each cup
bobbing on the surface
like life jackets
until they sink of their own weight and wetness
I watch the milk swirl into the mixture
and imagine the sugar releasing its sweetness
yes
something was stirred here
and leaves a picture I freeze with my eyes
until some time passes
and I tie the two threads together
like a tightrope and balance my self
over the rising steam

Wildlife Via Canada

From the train I saw
that the trees went down to the lake
or was it that the lake
came up to the trees;
I pressed my face
against the window looking for
signs of wildlife like moose or
beaver while the hours passed

and I ate an orange and peanuts
and whenever the train slowed
I searched again for the wildlife
promised in the travel guide;
nothing moved--although
once I saw a tree felled by a
beaver, its point of separation
sharpened like a pencil

hunger overcame me;
I joined a table of other
strangers in the dining car;
we talked about the lack of wildlife

Suddenly a young man pointed
to the sky and said look--what a wingspan!
We agreed it was a hawk but later
I read the brochure again

and thought
it could have been an eagle
because that was what was promised

Night Dilemma I

I wonder if I should reach down to the foot
of the bed and pull up the extra blanket
or content myself with the heating pad;

If I content myself with the heating pad
and still get chilly during the night
and reach down for the extra blanket

I am afraid I will disturb the heating pad
that sits on my chest
like a cat.

Night Dilemma II

If I stay in bed and do not
get up and find paper and pen

In the morning I will not remember
what I wanted to remember

Instead, I will have an uneasy feeling that
it was something important

Something not remembered will haunt me
until I go to bed that night

And wonder anew
if the thought that escaped

will find its way back again
Now that I have paper and pen

Dream Life

He leaves a note on his pillow
"Can't sleep. Have gone for a run."
Wraps sneakers loosely around his neck
Runs barefoot through moonlit snow

She sits at the kitchen table, writing
"Can't sleep. We need milk. Have gone to find
some open place."

They meet at the all-night diner;
He orders coffee for them both
They laugh about frozen toes

She warms his feet
between her thighs
and before dawn
they sip the steam
from each other's eyes

Shopping for Peaches

I wear cutoffs and a loose top
A man nearby--shorts and sandals
A woman looks hot in a sleeveless dress

What does it matter what we wear?
In summer's heat, we are almost bare;
We barely notice each other

Lost in sensual thought
Feeling the soft peach skin in our hands
Like carefree lovers caressing thighs

Firewood

If you know anyone who needs firewood,
tell them to come
here

Dry branches, easily snapped,
tossed into a garden cart
rolled down the hill

dumped near the creek
the other side of the road
Load after load

I imagine some distant country
where weary women
carry hungry babies wrapped in rags

beg for wood
to cook flatbread or
mush over a small fire

Imagine them pleading
offering their shrouds,
bracelets, anything for this wood

Such thoughts cross my mind
like fallen limbs on soft carpets of periwinkle
near quiet daffodils

If you know anyone who needs firewood,
please tell them
many branches are here

On Seeing the Universe
In a Blade of Grass

"It was a dandelion choked me,"
she said.

"No," he said, "It was a ruffle."

"No, it was a dandelion choked me,"
she said. "I was down on my knees
looking for the universe
in a blade of grass.

"I asked the sun to let some light in.
Then I fell into a black hole and came up
spewing dandelion seeds. And the wind
took them everywhere."

"It was a ruffle," he said,
crossing her arms in front of her
and tying long strings
around her universe.

The Muted Town Crier

Paper place mats are easily torn
(Two pieces for the eyes)

Look at this face, just born
(One piece each for the nose and mouth)

This habit plagues my diner years
(Two scraps for the ears)

I could sweep this paper doodle to the floor
(Swap the nose for one eye)

But doodling lives in my unconscious hands
(Satisfied yet?)

Go on now! Open your mouth of shred!
(I can't)

Say what you came to tell!
(I can't speak)

Say: "I am the muted town crier; All Is Not Well."
(All Is Not Well)

The Tapes

It's not like these were playthings, you know
toys you threw away when they
were broken or overused

These were tapes—audio tapes
by people who cared about what they were
reading aloud or singing about

And now when you finger the old tapes--
even if you could find a machine that still worked--
the tape breaks in your hand

piece by piece
brittle, like dried leaves
no life left.

There's a saying, "It's not carved
in stone, you know."
I know. You can't bring that voice

back from the brittle tape
not like Edison's wire
or hieroglyphics on a cave wall

If everything were carved in stone
sure, it would probably last forever
But then who would want to live like that?

word after word
carved onto rocks
next to each other

If you lost your place in the story
You'd have to walk back half a mile
just to find the beginning of the sentence.

Famous Author Reads

Afterwards, I joined the line to buy her newest book
She signed each as if from a distance

Some students nearby talked excitedly,
her reading had stimulated them, awakened them

I stared at the stack of her books;
suddenly the books fell over; no one was near

One student saw it happen and wanted an interview;
she believed I caused this disturbance

She asked where I had learned to move things
without touching them--

Truth be told, I said,
when I was young I admired a cartoonist

who drew ordinary people
doing ordinary things

while their shadows
did something mischievous

Missed Photo Op # 1
Rome Railway Station, Summer 1985

She in a white dress
He in a uniform
She with her hair down her back
He with a gun slung over his shoulder
She slightly up on her toes
He bent over near her lips
She with her arms around his neck
He with his arms around her waist
She waiting
He wanting

Missed Photo Op # 2
Newburyport, Summer 1994

I saw him through the cafe window
    walking across the cobblestone square
    saw him open a small case
    bring out a music stand and a flute
    and begin to play

The swinging cafe door was closed but
    when someone came in or went out
    I could hear the melody rising and falling;
    after that he was like a mime
    twisting and turning in the sun

Missed Photo Op # 3
Winter, Poughkeepsie

She opened the trunk of her car;
he sat in the shopping cart
a giant white stuffed dog
with stitched eyes and nose
towering over her
looking like he wanted to bark.

She tossed her scarf back around
her neck and rearranged the objects
in the trunk to make room
for one more.

He looked regal,
unmoving,
acrylic fur trapping snowflakes

How to Learn To Sing

First, find the song that

lives in your heart

How to Begin To Exercise

Say good morning

to your toes

How to Begin to Write--
Try the Alphabet List

About	Nuance
Beginnings	Openings
Caring	Pain
Determination	Questions
Energy	Rehearsals
Frustrations	Stretching
Grasping	Thirst
Holding	Understanding
Intuition	Visualizing
Jams	Weeping
Kisses	X-Rays
Listening	Yearning
Metaphors	Zeniths

How to Continue to Write--
Try the Alphabet Sentence

A burden
candidly described
eventually finds
grateful healing
inside, justified
knowing love
means never
owning people,
quietly raising
stuck touchstones
undying visions
winged xylophones
yes Zest!

Writing Prompt
(dream)

A headstone says

> ***Here in***
> ***Lies***
> ***Possibilities***

Sister Fear
    (dream)

She insists that the diving
board is not too high--

That she can climb the ladder
and walk to the end, jump or dive--

I insist that she must not try it,
that she is too heavy

Too uncertain of her balance
that she might trip before reaching the end

Or slip sideways
and, and, what then? What then?

On a Letter of Rejection

After that letter came,
I saw geese flying out of formation
calling to each other
scrambling to make a V.

Nearby
a cardinal on a feeder
swayed in the wind
shifting balance to maintain balance;

Nothing is perfect;
the stone from my ring
lost somewhere on a sandy beach
perhaps covered by sand or water,

perhaps found by a seeker of shells.
I wear the ring anyway,
a reminder to look
beyond disappointment,

to observe how geese scramble and squawk
until they find their place again;

how a cardinal perched in its cocoon of red
dropped to the ground for scattered seeds;

I would have missed all that
if my mood was different,
if I were not reflecting on arrow patterns in the sky
or how a winter cardinal warms my blood

Have I ever told you
that I have grown to love that
space where the slender turquoise stone
once graced my ring?

It speaks to me of
possibilities, of new arrangements;
it suggests stories of wings that soar
and wings that wait.

When I was Eight

My brother said
it could happen here
I lie awake
frozen with fear
feeling my skin
what would I answer when
they struck the door
Juden?
Out!

I hear cries so far away I
cannot place them;
my mother said it's my imagination
my father said it's the wind
my brother waited until nightfall
and told me again
what he heard in school
about lamp shades and skin

The next day near home--
allowed to ride bareback--
I am lifted high onto a gentle horse;
I feel cool sweat beneath my knees

hug the horse's neck, hold the rein
my soft cheek against a coarse mane
laughing tears, waving to my brother
as we ride past the tall trees,

and the wind brushes my thick braids
back so free
pushing away those mysterious cries.

Somewhere there was a parting kiss
I was too young to know

somewhere, far away
soldiers hissed
Juden?
Out!

my brother said it could happen here
when I was eight.

Whose Lint Between Her Toes

Startles me,
who is my daughter first born
who sits on my lap
while I read of poverty in
Wye, Virginia
where another child sits in excrement
three days down her legs.

My baby,
whose lint between her toes
moves me to quick action
whose father kisses her belly
while I remove the lint.
She of our common joy
too young to sit up alone in her tub

While I, just as helpless,
think about bathing another baby
lying under a rag
on a cold floor
in Wye, Virginia.

Lullaby

My daughter is almost two
My son not quite two months
he is in his bassinet
forefinger on his chin, deep in thought

His dark hair still damp from his bath
his favorite rag unfurled near his cheek
I kiss his forehead, his eyelids flutter,
I begin my lullaby; he falls asleep

My daughter waits patiently in her crib
I kiss her forehead, smooth her red hair
she reaches up, twirls my own long hair
I close my eyes, pretending sleep

When I open them, she smiles up at me
I yawn, then restart my lullaby
how it is time to sleep
how the good things will keep

Till tomorrow comes around
Till tomorrow comes around

Grammar Lesson: To, Two, and Too

Stay with her
because she wants you to
because she's only two
because you too may be afraid someday
when she is in another room
and seems so far away.

The Present

My little children want to see
what I hide in the palm of my hand
want to know if it is a gift for them
and after much struggle
and laughter I let them
pry open my fingers
and I look up
as if something flew away
and the children run after it
and soon return
to search my hand again
to look for some trace
and I can see that they are
puzzled by the
smile on my face

Elegy for My Father

I remember riding high on his shoulders
hugging his chin shouting into the wind
"Diddy up, Daddy! Diddy up!"

I remember how different he looked
coming home from the hospital
after an accident shattered more than his arm;

I remember how his face became like a mask;
how Parkinson's slowed his gait,
how every task was a triumph of mind over body;

I remember when he fell in the bathroom
and I ran upstairs and walked him
back to his bed, how he cried;

I remember my mother shaving him, dressing him
easing him into his reading chair,
watching his hands shake holding *Think* magazine;

I remember the night she telephoned me
I remember the sound of her voice
the long, unintelligible, breathless wail and I knew;

I remember how we tended his grave site,
how she reminded me where her urn was to go
on the shoulder of his casket;

I remember kissing the simple stone where both lie,
whispering news of children and grandchildren
—as if asked;

I remember that lawn again
between the house and the bungalow,
riding high on my father's shoulders;

I remember holding on to his chin,
I remember my voice shouting into the wind
"Diddy up, Daddy. Diddy up!"

Elegy for My Mother: Hand to Hand

You said I had beautiful hands;
then you looked pensively at your own
worn to the bone washing dishes and clothes

You said I could be a hand model;
I said I was not interested;
Maybe the hands of a poet? I asked

Then you smiled, a change of mood;
Your double-jointed index finger playfully
trying to lie straight

I laughed, asked you to do that again
Do that again!
How did you do that?

Decades later, after a massive stroke
you lie motionless;
Only one finger moved—that double jointed one;

--it rubbed methodically across the sheet;
I stroked your hand, held that finger carefully,
Filed the rough nail edge

Still it seemed not to beckon as before--
Like Poe's Raven, Nevermore;
I lay my hand on top of yours

Hoping to calm your motionless body,
Your eyes, gray green
Darting around the room

I asked, Do you know my name?
Blink once for no, twice for yes
I said my sister's name. One blink. No.

I said my own name. Two blinks. Yes!
Then you curved your hand slightly and
with great effort, you made a small wave

A wave of goodbye to me
Goodbye to all your children and grandchildren
goodbye, goodbye...

...As my own years unfold I notice that
the less slender, the bumpier my fingers,
the more poems I am able to write.

Tree

We carry you indoors at holiday time
fresh cut, your branches tickle.

Is the warm air another death to you
the way we naked are numbed by cold?

Soon bright lights will circle
your fragrant boughs;

Soon you will be dressed in
layers of old and new trimmings;

Then we will admire
the fullness of your branches;

We will say--
what a beautiful tree

Your mute
trunk
sipping water

To Be A Poet

means
the soft
green needle
from an evergreen
can sew words to
your universe
and
bend
you

Sydna Altschuler Byrne

is a writer, editor, and communications consultant. She began her career at WGBH in Boston and after graduate school, became an editor at Beacon Press. Later, moving to Denver, she edited the University of Colorado Medical School Quarterly and the Medical Center News. Back east, in addition to free-lance writing, she edited publications for the Hudson River Sloop Clearwater and Oakwood Friends School. Sydna also taught college writing and designed and led hundreds of communication skills workshops--including business and technical writing, and public speaking--for Marist College, Dutchess Community College, IBM, and others.

Writing for the theater included StageWorks equity productions of several one-act plays ("The Second Arrow" and "Studying Crows"). Sydna's adaptation of the classic short story "The Yellow Wallpaper" (Gilman) was co-produced by the Cunneen-Hackett Arts Center and DAWN (Directors, Actors, Writers Network).

Previous publications include *Wings That Wait* (Finishing Line Press), *Foods From Mother Earth* (Shawangunk) and *Haiku: Two Butterflies Dance* (Epigraph). Sydna has two degrees from Boston University (BA, American Literature; MS, Journalism).

A native New England-er, Sydna lives in Poughkeepsie, NY, with her husband, William. They have two loving children and four lively grandchildren.

www.ingramcontent.com/pod-product-compliance
Lightning Source LLC
Chambersburg PA
CBHW051703040426
42446CB00009B/1276